make it in
Minutes

Party Favors
& Hostess Gifts

make it in
Minutes

Party Favors
& Hostess Gifts

ROXI PHILLIPS

A Division of Sterling Publishing Co., Inc. New York

Book Editor
Catherine Risling

Copy Editor
Lisa Anderson

Photographer
Zachary Williams
Williams Visual
Ogden, UT

Stylist
Brittany Aardema

Book Designer
Kehoe + Kehoe Design
Associates, Inc.
Burlington, VT

*Other Books
in this Series:*

Make It in Minutes:
Greeting Cards

Make It in Minutes:
Mini-Books

Make It in Minutes:
Mini-Boxes

Make It in Minutes:
Beaded Jewelry

A Red Lips 4 Courage Communications, Inc. book
www.redlips4courage.com
Eileen Cannon Paulin
President
Catherine Risling
Director of Editorial

10 9 8 7 6 5 4 3 2 1
First Edition

Published by Lark Books, A Division of
Sterling Publishing Co., Inc.
387 Park Avenue South, New York, NY 10016

Text © 2007, Roxi Phillips
Photography © 2007, Lark Books
Illustrations © 2007, Lark Books

Distributed in Canada by Sterling Publishing,
c/o Canadian Manda Group, 165 Dufferin Street
Toronto, Ontario, Canada M6K 3H6

Distributed in the United Kingdom by GMC Distribution Services,
Castle Place, 166 High Street, Lewes, East Sussex, England BN7 1XU

Distributed in Australia by Capricorn Link (Australia) Pty Ltd.,
P.O. Box 704, Windsor, NSW 2756 Australia

If you have questions or comments about this book, please contact:
Lark Books
67 Broadway
Asheville, NC 28801
(828) 253-0467

Manufactured in China
All rights reserved

ISBN 13: 978-1-60059-126-6
ISBN 10: 1-60059-126-4

For information about custom editions, special sales, premium, and corporate purchases, please contact Sterling Special Sales Department at (800) 805-5489 or specialsales@sterlingpub.com.

"Every gift from a friend
is a wish for your happiness."
—Richard Bach

Baby Shower Favors

Hostess Gifts

Wedding Favors

Contents

Introduction

Celebrations fill our hearts, whether we are the guest of honor, the party giver, or an attendee. Unique party favors are meaningful touches that guests will enjoy long after the refreshments are gone and the festivities are over. These personal mementos range from tiny tokens of appreciation to props for a party to clever gifts that double as table decorations. As a guest at one of these memorable occasions, a gracious gesture is to bring something special to the hostess. In this book you will find an array of creative favors and thoughtful gifts for a variety of parties. With a few simple supplies, some basic techniques, and intriguing packaging, you are on your way to creating party favors and hostess gifts with a personal touch that will surely leave a lasting impression long after the party is over.

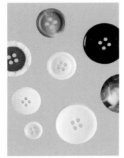

CHAPTER 1

When preparing to entertain guests at a social gathering or celebration, begin by thinking about the theme or the type of event. Consider the attendees' personalities and the atmosphere you hope to create. From there, plan the details, including a memento to give each of your guests. Familiarize yourself with the basic techniques, tools, and supplies in this chapter and you will be well equipped to create handmade party favors your visitors will treasure long after the last dance is over or the last piece of cake is eaten. Use these same techniques and tools to create beautiful gifts for the hostesses of parties and celebrations you are invited to attend. They are fun to create and enjoyable to give.

Getting Started

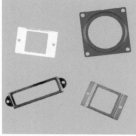
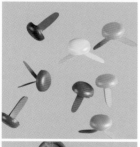
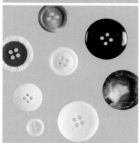

Embellishments

Acrylic paint

Acrylic paint applied with a foam brush or in a dabber adds color to your projects. Can also be applied to rubber stamps that are pressed onto surfaces. An alternative medium, spray paints come in a variety of colors and textures, providing a quick and thorough application.

Beads

Beads add an elegant touch to any project. String them in a pleasing pattern on craft wire for a dimensional accent. Applying beads directly onto paper or projects requires the use of beading glue or tacky tape for a strong bond.

Bookplates

Bookplates are label holders attached to a project with a brad on either side. A paper label is inserted into the top of the plate.

Brads

Brads are readily available at craft and hobby stores. You'll find them in all colors, shapes, and sizes. They can be used to hold elements in place or as decorations on their own. Simply push them through a pre-punched hole and then spread open the prongs and flatten to the back to secure.

Buttons

Use buttons as a finishing touch on handmade projects. They can suggest a closure or provide the perfect embellishment. Adhere buttons to projects with craft glue or glue dots.

Cellophane sheets and bags

Cellophane can be purchased in rolls or as pre-made bags in a variety of sizes. Wrap favors or gifts in cellophane and add a decorative tie, or fill bags with goodies to be inserted into a themed party package.

Chalks

Use chalks to create soft colors and shading using cosmetic sponges, cotton balls, or cotton swabs. This versatile medium can be used wet or dry. It is easy to age a paper element, create soft backgrounds, add shading to die cuts or stamped images, or highlight elements.

Charms

There are charms to match any party theme. Made from a variety of materials including metal and plastic, charms can be attached to a project with glue dots or can be dangled from ribbons, fibers, or craft wire.

Chenille stems

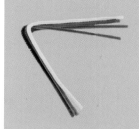

Commonly known as pipe cleaners, these stems have a wire center and are covered with chenille. Twist them around a pencil to create spirals or gather around wrapping paper to secure it closed.

Craft wire

This versatile product comes in a wide variety of colors and gauges. Can be used to string beads, create spirals, or to secure embellishments to party favors.

Decorative paper

Paper is available in a wide variety of colors, types, weights, and textures. Can be adhered using practically any type of adhesive. When using vellum, vellum adhesive tape works best.

Die-cuts

Typically made of cardstock or heavy paper, die-cuts are printed with a sentiment or cut into themed shapes. Do-it-yourself systems are readily available and dies come in a vast array of styles.

time-saving tip

Assembly-Line Crafting

When creating numerous favors for an event, make all components of the project and then put them together in assembly-line fashion.

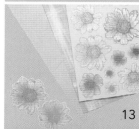

Embossing powder

Embossing powder, when heated on a surface, adds a beautifully dimensional appearance to stamped images. It comes in many colors, granule sizes, and textures to complement any project.

Fabric

Textiles are an excellent way to add depth and warmth to a party favor or hostess gift. Most patterned fabrics lend themselves well to photocopying to create custom papers. Adhere fabric using glue dots, foam mounting dots, craft glue, or a hot glue gun and glue sticks.

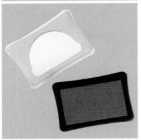

Inkpads

There are a variety of inks in pads, and each has a different purpose. Dye inks dry quickly and work well on paper. Permanent ink can be used on non-porous surfaces as well as paper. All inks can be used directly from the pad or applied to a rubber stamp and pressed onto a surface.

Jewels

Add glamour and sparkle to your party favors with these little gems. Adhere to projects with craft glue or glue dots.

Leafing pens

Leafing pens are metal-barreled pens that dispense paint, rather than ink, through a felt tip. Metallic gold, silver, and copper leafing pens can be used to color metal embellishments such as brads.

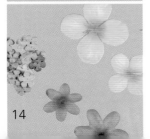

Paper and silk botanicals

Flowers and leaves bring an organic appeal to your projects and are readily available in every color of the rainbow. Attach botanicals to a party favor by tying in place, adhering with craft glue or glue dots, or securing with brads.

time-saving tip

At the Ready

Gathering all tools and supplies before beginning a project will allow you to create favors in minutes.

Ribbon

Use ribbon as an embellishment or to secure projects. Tie bows or knots or secure directly with adhesive.

Rub-ons

These adhesive decals are applied to the surface of a project using a craft stick. Available in numerous colors, images, fonts, and styles, rub-ons are a simple way to add a decorative touch.

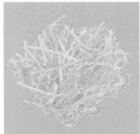

Shredded paper

Available in many colors, shredded paper adds to the festive feel of a party favor when spilling from the gift. Use as a base for small gifts.

Spanish moss

Spanish moss comes in a variety of natural colors and works well as filler for gardening or other nature-themed favors or gifts. Can be adhered to projects with craft glue.

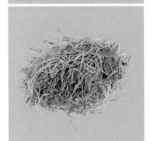

Stickers

From alphabet letters to any other theme imaginable, stickers are a quick and easy way to add interest and detail to your party favors and hostess gifts.

Test tube

A test tube is a piece of laboratory glassware composed of a finger-like length of glass tubing that is open at the top, with a rounded base. Test tubes can double as a vase or, when corked at the top, they can hold granules such as sea salts.

Additional Supplies

There are many everyday items that will help you craft and embellish party favors and hostess gifts, including:

- Binder clips
- Computer and printer
- Copier
- Copy paper
- Paper clips
- Pencil
- Rubber bands
- Safety pins
- Scrap paper
- Straight pins
- Twine
- Wax paper

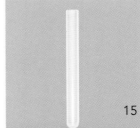

Tools

Awl

Bone folder

Colored pencils

Cosmetic sponges

Craft knife

Craft mat

Craft scissors

Craft stick

Decorative-edge scissors

Dowel

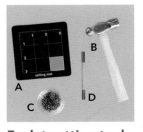

Eyelet setting tools
A Setting mat   C Eyelets
B Craft hammer   D Eyelet setter

Foam brushes

Heat tool

Hole punch

Hot glue gun

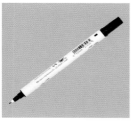

Journaling pen

Metal-edge ruler

Paper punch

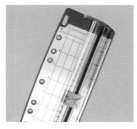

Paper trimmer

Rubber stamps

Sandpaper

Scoring tool

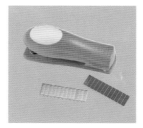

Stapler and staples

Wire pliers

Adhesives

Acid-free tape runner

Cellophane tape

Clear packing tape

Foam mounting dots

Foam tape

Glitter glue

Glue dots

Glue stick

Hot glue sticks

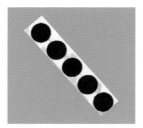

Self-adhesive hook-and-loop dots

Vellum tape

White craft glue

Techniques

Adhering craft jewels

Roll a small ball of beeswax and attach it to the end of a piercing tool or toothpick. Place a small amount of craft glue on a piece of cardboard. Pick up jewel by pressing the beeswax onto the top of the stone. Dip the stone back lightly into the glue, wiping off excess glue on the cardboard. Place the jewel as desired and then remove it from the tool by pressing lightly on the jewel with your fingernail or tweezers.

Applying rub-ons

Rub-ons come on a transfer sheet and often contain several images. Carefully cut out the chosen image. Position on the project and firmly rub the image with a craft stick or rub-on tool until it is completely transferred. Carefully lift one corner and pull the backing off slowly, assuring a successful transfer.

Beading

Craft wire, pliers, and beads are all readily available at craft stores. A few lovely beads in coordinating colors strung on wire can embellish party favors and hostess gifts and add an interesting dimensional element. Strips of adhesive paper covered in seed beads make a beautiful border accent on any project.

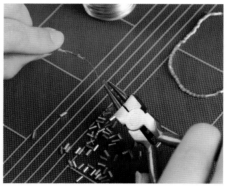

Computer printing on scrapbook paper

To print onto scrapbook paper, trim paper to 8½" x 11" and print as usual. It is a good idea to print onto computer paper first to check the image, and then print onto the decorative paper to ensure exact placement of wording. Follow the printer manual for specific instructions.

time-saving tip

Having Gifts on Hand

When creating a hostess gift, make a few extras while you have all the tools and supplies together. It will be nice to have them on hand for future events.

Heat embossing

Embossing creates a raised effect on a stamped image. Stamp an image with clear embossing ink or pigmented ink then cover ink with embossing powder. Tap off excess powder. Carefully wipe away any remaining embossing powder with a small, soft brush, avoiding image. Heat powder using a heat tool until melted, forming a hard surface.

Inking edges

Give your projects a finished look by inking the exposed cut edges of paper. Simply tap the inkpad around the edge of the paper to give a subtle framed effect, or ink more heavily for a distressed appearance. For a softer look, apply ink by patting a cosmetic sponge onto the inkpad and then dabbing the sponge lightly onto the edges or surfaces of the paper.

Matting images or text boxes

Cut a piece of coordinating paper at least ⅛" larger than the object to be matted. Center and adhere the object onto the mat. For additional flair, the object may be matted more than once, or edges can be trimmed with decorative-edge scissors.

Rubber stamping images

Basic stamping is pretty simple. Pat a stamp image firmly onto the surface of an inkpad. Position inked stamp above area to be stamped and press it firmly onto surface. Lift stamp off surface without smearing ink. Most permanent inks only take a few seconds to dry. If needed, heat surface with a heat tool to set ink.

Scoring paper

Score paper by laying a metal-edge ruler on the edge of the line to be scored and running a hard smooth-edged tool, such as a bone folder or scoring tool, along the score line. This will ensure a smooth, neatly folded edge on your project. Scoring boards and score blades are also readily available and work well.

Setting eyelets

To set eyelets in paper, punch a small hole in the paper where the eyelet is to be set. Insert the eyelet through the hole and position the project face down on a craft mat. Using a setting tool and hammer, flatten the eyelet's backside to secure it in place. *Note:* Some eyelet setting systems vary; simply follow the manufacturer's instructions.

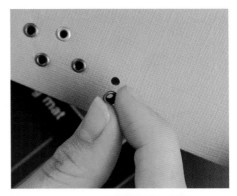

Working with wire

Use the needle nose of wire pliers to help bend wire into the desired shapes. Wire pliers also double as wire cutters when the wire is pushed close to the hinge. Very thin wire can be cut with craft scissors.

Tearing paper edges

To achieve an organic feel, it's best to tear your handmade papers rather than cut them. Be sure to test-tear a sample before tearing the actual project paper.

Instructions

1. To tear a straight line, paint a line of water to weaken the paper where you want it to tear.

2. Hold edge of desired paper, and with a hand on either side of the area to be torn, pull one side toward you. The paper edge will differ depending on which side you pull.

CHAPTER 2

Watching the wide-eyed excitement of children at a party is as much fun as planning and preparing for the celebration itself. Your young guests will be excited to open their very own gifts when you adorn their place settings with any of the favors you'll find on the following pages. From presents that double as centerpieces to the charming presentation of treats, these favors will delight children as they feel just as special as the guest of honor. Check out the fascinating packaging of the favors in a bottle and the circlets with flowing ribbons—the treasures in this chapter are sure to bring a twinkle to the eyes of all the youngsters and add joy to the festivities.

Children's Party Favors

Princess Circlet

Materials

- Adhesive: hot glue sticks
- Craft scissors
- Hoop: 6"-8" wire or wooden
- Hot glue gun
- Ribbons: ¼" white satin; ⅜" organdy (2 coordinating)
- Ruler
- Silk flowers: 20 small with wire stems

Instructions

1. Place drop of hot glue on hoop and attach end of 3-yard length of white satin ribbon. Wrap hoop with ribbon until hoop is completely covered, applying dot of hot glue every 2".

2. Evenly space flowers and wrap wire around covered hoop. *Note:* Dried flowers, sequins, or beads could be substituted for silk flowers and hot glued in place.

3. Cut four 5' lengths of organdy ribbons; fold ribbons in half then knot onto backside of hoop. *Note:* For a fuller look, add more ribbons.

time-saving tip

Painter's Choice

Hoops may be spray painted with acrylic or glitter paint instead of wrapped with ribbon to save time.

Fairy Wand

Materials

- Adhesives: cellophane tape, craft glue, glitter glue
- Binder clips
- Craft foam sheets
- Craft jewels
- Craft scissors
- Heat tool
- Necklace: children's costume jewelry
- Ribbon: $\frac{1}{4}$" curling
- Rubber stamp: large background image
- Ruler
- Spray paint: glossy white
- Wooden bead: 1" with $\frac{1}{4}$" hole
- Wooden dowel: $\frac{1}{4}$" x 18"

Instructions

1. Spray dowel and wooden bead with glossy white paint; let dry. Wrap dowel with curling ribbon in a spiral from top to bottom and secure with tape.

2. Cut two stars from craft foam using Fairy Wand Template (page 118). Heat foam star with heat tool one side at a time; quickly press rubber stamp into hot foam, leaving impression. Embellish star fronts with glitter glue and craft jewels; let dry.

3. Cut five 2' lengths of ribbon. Tape ends to top end of dowel; curl ribbons by carefully running along edge of scissor blade.

4. Sandwich top end of dowel and three strands of beaded necklace between foam stars; adhere together with generous amount of craft glue. Hold together with binder clips until completely dry.

5. Add bit of craft glue to bottom of dowel and then insert into painted bead.

time-saving tip

Glitter Instead of Stamp

Rather than making impressions into the foam stars, simply embellish with glitter and glue.

My Stuff Box

Materials

- Adhesive: tape runner
- Cardstock: double-sided
- Cosmetic sponge
- Craft scissors
- Decorative paper
- Hole punches: 1¼", 1½"
- Inkpad: permanent
- Journaling pen: white
- Metal box: bandage-style with handle
- Ribbons: ¼" coordinating colors (5-6)
- Ruler

Instructions

1. Sponge permanent ink on lid of box. Measure, cut, and adhere decorative paper around body of box with tape runner.

2. Punch circles from both sides of cardstock using paper punches; layer and adhere together. Draw dots around edges of circle with journaling pen; adhere to front of box.

3. Cut eleven ribbons to 6"; tie to handle, alternating colors.

time-saving tip

Go Wide with Ribbons

Embellishing the handle with fewer but wider ribbons will save time while still lending the My Stuff Box a playful look.

Favors in a Bottle

Materials

- Adhesives: clear packing tape, tape runner
- Cosmetic sponge
- Craft knife
- Craft scissors
- Decorative paper: coordinating colors (3)
- Die-cut letters: 1"
- Filler: small toys or candy
- Inkpad: coordinating color
- Plastic bottle: one-liter
- Ribbons: ⅜" coordinating colors (2)
- Ruler
- Shredded paper: coordinating color

Instructions

1. Cut one-liter bottle in half across center of bottle using craft knife; wash and dry thoroughly.

2. Fill bottom of bottle half with shredded paper and small toys or candy, making sure favors show through bottle. Attach top half with clear packing tape.

3. **To make label:** Cut coordinating decorative paper into 11" x 3½", 11" x 2", and 11" x 1" strips; ink all edges using cosmetic sponge. Arrange paper strips on flat surface and adhere together using tape runner. Adhere die-cut letters to center of paper strips; tie 3" length of ribbon to one letter. Adhere layered paper around center of bottle, covering packing tape.

4. Adhere two 4" pieces of coordinating ribbon around neck of bottle to hide threads. Insert shredded paper into top, allowing it to "flow" out.

time-saving tip

Fill It with Fun

Treats don't have to be candy. Consider filling plastic bottles with bouncy balls, glow-in-the-dark stars, marbles, or jacks.

Art Bucket

Materials

- Acrylic paint
- Adhesive: double-sided tape
- Bucket: 4"
- Cardstock: solid color
- Craft scissors
- Crayons: assorted colors (4)
- Hole punch: ¼" circle
- Pencil with new eraser
- Ribbon: ¼" grosgrain (1 yard)
- Shredded paper
- Stickers: 1" alphabet, birthday-themed

Instructions

1. Personalize bucket with child's name using alphabet stickers. Apply acrylic paint dots using eraser end of pencil as applicator; let dry.

2. To make party hat: Copy Art Bucket Template (page 118) onto cardstock; cut out. Punch hole with hole punch 4" in from straight edges and ½" up from rounded bottom edge. Roll hat shape into tube and tie with 18" length of grosgrain ribbon.

3. Bundle crayons and tie with 18" length of grosgrain ribbon. *Note:* Both ribbon lengths will be used later as party hat ties and therefore should not be trimmed.

4. Fill bucket with shredded paper, birthday-themed stickers, party hat, and crayon bundle. *Note:* Children will use stickers and crayons to embellish their own party hats.

5. When hats are decorated, overlap straight edges by ½" and adhere with double-sided tape. Tie ribbon to each side of hat through holes.

time-saving tip

Change Bucket Decor

Instead of painting the bucket, allow children to decorate their own bucket as well as their party hats. Just supply the decorative paper and craft glue and see what they can do.

Party Popper

Materials

- Adhesives: cellophane tape, foam dots
- Cardstock
- Chenille stems (4)
- Decorative paper
- Filler: candies, confetti, small gifts
- Inkpad: coordinating color
- Paper punch: 2" circle
- Paper tube: 4½"
- Pencil
- Rubber stamps: alphabet
- Ruler
- Scissors: craft, decorative-edge
- Tissue paper

Instructions

1. Tightly roll paper tube down center of 12"-square piece of tissue paper; secure with tape.

2. Twist one end of tissue paper and secure with two chenille stems. Fill opposite end with gifts, candies, and confetti; twist closed and secure with remaining two chenille stems. Wrap chenille stems around pencil to create spirals.

3. Cut piece of decorative paper to 4"x6"; trim 6" edge with decorative-edge scissors. Wrap decorative paper around center of tube and secure with tape.

4. Stamp word or child's name on cardstock and cut out with circle punch; adhere to tube with foam dots.

time-saving tip

Speed up the Process

One 12"-square sheet of decorative paper will make six poppers. To make multiple poppers quickly, use a paper trimmer to cut the paper.

Knapsack

Materials

- Adhesive: craft glue
- Bandana
- Corrugated cardboard
- Cosmetic sponge
- Craft scissors
- Eyelet
- Eyelet setting tools
- Filler: flashlight (optional), treats of choice
- Inkpads: black, brown
- Pencil
- Rubber stamps: alphabet, chicken wire
- Ruler
- Shredded paper
- Twig: 18" with "Y" at one end
- Twine

Instructions

1. Wrap 4" of twig with twine beginning 1" from end opposite "Y" end, adhering with craft glue as you wrap; let dry.

2. Lay bandana on table and fill with shredded paper and treats. Gather corners and knot onto "Y" end of twig.

3. **To create tag:** Cut corrugated cardboard to 4" x 2½". Randomly tear off top layer of cardboard, partly exposing middle layer. Stamp with chicken wire image and ink edges with brown ink using cosmetic sponge. Stamp child's name with alphabet stamps and black ink.

4. Set eyelet in upper left corner of tag. Tie tag to bandana knot with twine.

time-saving tip

Fill with Tummy Stuffers

If the knapsack party favor is for a sleepover, you may want to fill it with late-night snacks so small guests can help themselves when hunger strikes.

Tic-Tac-Toe Tin

Materials

- Adhesives: glue dots, tape runner
- Buttons: $\frac{1}{2}$" two colors (4 each)
- Cardstock: white
- Computer and printer
- Cosmetic sponge
- Craft scissors
- Decorative paper: coordinating patterns (2)
- Fiber (1 yard)
- Hole punch: $\frac{1}{2}$"
- Inkpad: coordinating color
- Magnetic sheet
- Mint tin
- Paper punches: corner rounder
- Pencil: 3"
- Ruler
- Sticker strips
- Sticky note pad: $1\frac{1}{2}$" x 2"

Instructions

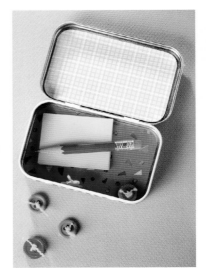

1. Cut four pieces of decorative paper to $3\frac{1}{2}$" x $2\frac{1}{8}$"; round all corners with corner rounder. Using tape runner, adhere to inside and outside of tin lid and base.

2. Embellish outside edges of tin with sticker strips. Measure and mark tic-tac-toe grid with $\frac{3}{4}$" squares toward right side of tin lid; place sticker strips on grid.

3. Using computer, print "Tic Tac Toe" onto white cardstock. Cut out each word, ink edges using cosmetic sponge, and adhere to lid using tape runner.

4. Thread fiber through holes of buttons; tie and trim excess. Punch $\frac{1}{2}$" circles from magnetic sheet. Apply magnetic circle to underside of each button using glue dots. *Note:* Magnetic sheets may be cut with scissors.

5. Place sticky note pad and mini pencil inside base of tin. Attach buttons to tin.

CHAPTER 3

Good friends, good food, good fun… a recipe for a successful party, for sure, but add the perfect personalized party favor and you'll have a celebration that will be the talk of the town. Pamper your guests with beautifully packaged soaps, provide a survival kit for those late-night scrapbooking events, highlight a "girl's night in" with a movie pack, or get the party started with coffee and rich, decadent chocolate. These fun and useful gifts will let your friends know how glad you are to have them at your party and in your life. The projects in this chapter will add another element to your gathering, providing lasting memories of good times shared with great friends.

Movie Night Box

Materials

- Acrylic paint
- Adhesive: tape runner
- Cardstock
- Craft scissors
- Decorative paper: coordinating prints (2)
- Filler: candy, microwave popcorn, movie rental gift card
- Foam brush
- Hole punch: ¼"
- Journaling pen
- Pencil
- Ribbon: ¼" curling
- Rubber stamp: circular label
- Sanding block
- Shredded paper
- Take-out box

Instructions

1. With wire handle in front, paint take-out box side and back panels with acrylic paint using foam brush; let dry. Stamp image on cardstock with paint to create circular label for tag; let dry, and then cut out. If desired, write guest's name on tag with journaling pen.

2. Using box as template, trace front panel and front flap onto decorative paper; cut two of each. Adhere paper pieces to inside back and outside front of box and inside front and back flaps. Sand edges.

3. Fold front flap onto box front, adhere tag to front flap, and punch two holes in front of tag. Thread curling ribbon through holes; tie and curl ends. *Note:* Back flap will remain standing to provide a backdrop.

4. Fill box with shredded paper and gift items.

time-saving tip

Pretty in Paint

Instead of covering the take-out box with decorative paper, purchase colored boxes or spray paint entire box.

Mulled Cider Packet

Materials

- Adhesives: glue dots, tape runner
- Bone folder
- Brads: small copper, square decorative
- Cardstock: pumpkin, rust
- Cellophane bag: 3"x4"
- Computer and printer
- Copper sheet
- Cosmetic sponge
- Craft scissors
- Decorative paper: autumn-themed
- Inkpads: dye inks in brown, red
- Leaf: silk
- Mulling spices: allspice berries (10), cardamom pods (4), cinnamon sticks (3), whole cloves (10)
- Paper punch: tag shape
- Pencil
- Ribbon: ⅜"-wide green
- Ruler
- Self-adhesive hook-and-loop dots: ½" circle
- Stapler and staples

Instructions

1. Copy Mulled Cider Packet Template (page 119) onto rust cardstock; cut out and score on solid lines according to template. Cut and adhere decorative paper to cover flap and 3" strip to lower section of packet front using tape runner. Ink all edges using brown ink and cosmetic sponge. Adhere 3" length of ribbon across front of packet.

2. Punch tag from copper sheet. Assemble tag and leaf; attach to packet front with copper brad.

time-saving tip

Paper Works Too

In place of copper sheeting, print "Autumn Greeting" onto metallic paper using a computer and cut into tag shape to embellish favor.

Mulled Cider

To the contents of the
spice packet add:

2 quarts apple cider
¼ cup firmly packed
light brown sugar

Combine all of the
ingredients in a large,
heavy pot over
medium-high heat.
Bring to a boil, then
reduce the heat and
simmer for five minutes.
Strain and serve hot.

Above: Beautifully crafted embellishments are readily available and add a sense of richness to projects. **Opposite:** A simple recipe is adhered to the inside of the packet with a tape runner.

3. Attach square brad to flap. Adhere hook-and-loop dot to underside of flap and front of folder.

4. Using computer, print Spiced Cider recipe (see page 46) onto pumpkin cardstock. Ink edges using red ink; adhere to inside back of packet.

5. Cut decorative paper to 3"x 4"; adhere to inside of bottom section.

6. Fill cellophane bag with mulling spices. Staple bag closed and cover staple with length of green ribbon tied into knot. Attach bag over decorative paper using glue dots.

time-saving tip

Filling with other Goodies

Rather than head to the store for cloves and cinnamon sticks, consider making this a Tea Time Packet or Lemonade Packet. You'll always save time when you simplify ingredients or use what you have on hand.

Scrapbook Survival Kit

Materials

- Adhesive: tape runner
- Brads (5)
- Computer and printer
- Computer paper
- Cosmetic sponge
- Craft scissors
- Decorative paper: double-sided
- Filler: bandages, chewing gum, chocolate
- Hole punch: $\frac{1}{8}$"
- Inkpad: coordinating color
- Matchboxes: small (5)
- Paper punch: $1\frac{3}{4}$" oval
- Ruler
- Spray paint: white glossy
- Twill tape: $\frac{3}{8}$"

Instructions

1. Empty matchboxes and separate "drawers" from "sleeves." Spray all sides of drawers with spray paint; let dry. Punch $\frac{1}{8}$" holes in front center of drawers; insert brads, opening prongs to secure. Insert drawers into sleeves.

2. Stack matchboxes and adhere with tape runner. Ink front and back edges of boxes using cosmetic sponge.

3. Cut strip of decorative paper to $2\frac{1}{8}$" x 8"; ink edges using cosmetic sponge. Wrap strip around stack of matchboxes and adhere in place, creasing well at corners.

4. Wrap 2' length of twill tape around box stack, tying bow on top. Punch oval from decorative paper; mat and punch $\frac{1}{8}$" hole in one end to create tag. Adhere tag next to bow.

time-saving tip

Consider Using Buttons

Save time by replacing the brads on the drawer fronts with small buttons adhered with glue dots.

Above and opposite: Filling the drawers with surprises will delight your guests.

5. Cut decorative paper to 1¼" x 5". Score and fold accordion style at 1¼" increments; ink edges using cosmetic sponge. Using computer, print desired phrases on computer paper in 1" x 1¼" text boxes such as: "A Scrapbook Survival Kit for You," "Chocolate to keep you going strong," "Bandages for your paper cuts," and "Chewing gum for fresh breath."

6. Fill drawers with chocolates, bandages, chewing gum, and quote strips. If desired, embellish drawer fronts with brads, buttons, or decorative clips.

time-saving tip

Matchboxes Come in White

Purchase white matchboxes from party supply stores to eliminate the need to spray paint the drawers.

Soap Wrapper

Materials

- Adhesive: tape runner
- Bar soap: rectangular or square
- Cardstock or handmade paper
- Craft scissors
- Decorative paper
- Embellishments: charms, tags, etc.
- Ribbon or hemp twine
- Ruler

Instructions

1. Cut cardstock to 2¾" x 8" and decorative paper to 2¼" x 8". Layer decorative paper on top of cardstock and wrap around bar of soap; adhere with tape runner. *Note:* Measurements may need to be altered to accommodate size of bar soap.

2. Tie with ribbon or twine; add embellishments as desired.

time-saving tip

Any Paper Will Do

Save scraps of paper strips for creating a variety of beautifully embellished soaps. Choose paper printed with stripes to give a layered effect with less effort. Soaps can be tied with ribbon, twine, fibers, or cord.

Spa Basket

Materials

- Adhesives: glue stick, tape runner
- Cardstock: coordinating color
- Craft scissors
- Decorative paper
- Filler: spa-related items
- Hole punches: ¼", ½"
- Inkpad: coordinating color
- Pencil
- Ribbon: ⅜"
- Rubber stamp: crown
- Ruler
- Scoring tool
- Shredded paper

Instructions

1. Copy Spa Basket Template (page 120); trace onto cardstock and cut out. Adhere cardstock to back side of decorative paper using glue stick; trim excess paper. Score along inside lines and crease.

2. Punch ¼" holes in outside corners of flaps. Thread four 6" lengths of ribbon through holes, bringing corners together to form basket.

3. Create labels for filler items by cutting strips of decorative paper to make bands; adhere in place using tape runner. Wrap and adhere ribbon around center of paper band. Punch three ½" circles from white cardstock; stamp crown image onto circles. Cut three ¾" squares from coordinating cardstock; adhere circles onto squares and squares onto filler bands.

4. Fill basket with shredded paper and spa-related items.

time-saving tip

Switch Out Your Paper

To save time, eliminate the need to adhere decorative paper to cardstock by using heavy double-sided printed cardstock.

Bath Salts

Materials

- Adhesive: tape runner
- Cardstock: off-white
- Corks (3)
- Cosmetic sponge
- Craft scissors
- Epsom salts
- Essential oils
- Eyelet
- Eyelet setting tools
- Food coloring
- Inkpad
- Paper with text
- Ruler
- Sea salt
- Test tubes (3)
- Twine

Instructions

1. Mix 2 parts Epsom salts, 1 part sea salt, 2–3 drops food coloring, and several drops essential oil; mix thoroughly. Repeat twice more with different color and fragrance combinations. Fill test tubes with bath salts; insert corks firmly at top.

2. Tear paper printed with text into 6" x ½" strips and wrap around test tubes; adhere with tape runner.

3. Cut cardstock into small strips and ink edges using cosmetic sponge; set eyelet near end of one of strips to use as a name tag, if desired. Adhere remaining strips to top of tubes. If desired, write names of essential oils on these strips.

4. Bundle test tubes together and wrap several times with twine, tying bow on front. String twine through eyelet on name strip; knot ends.

time-saving tip

Party Participation

Instead of mixing bath salts for your guests, provide a station where they can create their own unique scented salts to fill their test tubes.

Icicle Box

Materials

- Adhesive: ¼" double-sided tape
- Bone folder
- Button
- Cardstock: double-sided printed
- Cellophane bag: cone
- Chocolate-covered espresso beans
- Chocolate-dipped spoon
- Cosmetic sponge
- Craft scissors
- Hole punch: ⅜"
- Inkpad: coordinating color
- Pencil
- Ribbons: ⅜" organdy, 1" organdy
- Ruler
- Self-adhesive hook-and-loop dot: ½" circle

Instructions

1. Copy Icicle Box template (page 121); trace onto double-sided cardstock and cut out. Score and fold on all dashed lines; adhere narrow flap in place to form box. Ink all edges using cosmetic sponge.

2. Punch holes at center and ½" down from top edge of side sections. Cut 1" ribbon to 18" length; tie knot at one end and string ribbon through hole from inside box. Repeat on opposite side.

3. Embellish flap of cover with button adhered to outside and hook-and-loop dot to underside of flap and front of box.

4. Place espresso beans and chocolate-covered spoon in cellophane bag; tie with 12" length of ⅜" ribbon and insert into box. Tie ribbon in large bow on top of box.

time-saving tip

Leave Top Open
Leave the flap off the top of the Icicle Box to create an open container, which will allow favors to peek out and will eliminate the need for closure and button embellishments.

Personalized Votive

Materials

- Computer and printer
- Craft scissors
- Decorative paper
- Glass beads
- Glass votive holder
- Name plate label: 2¼"
- Ribbon: ⅞"
- Votive candle

Instructions

1. Form-fit name plate to glass votive holder by gently bending name plate around holder.

2. Using computer, print guest's name onto decorative paper if desired; cut to fit name plate and insert.

3. Thread 1 yard length of ribbon through both holes in name plate; wrap around votive and tighten ribbon. Bring ends of ribbon to back of votive and tie bow; trim ribbon ends.

4. Fill bottom of votive with glass beads; set candle inside holder.

time-saving tip

Replacing the Name Plate

For a quick alternative to the metal name plate, use stickers or stamp your guest's name on your choice of decorative paper.

CHAPTER 4

Welcome the little bundle of joy by throwing a baby shower for the parents to be. These clever ideas will add fun and excitement as you shower the baby with love and gifts. Your guests will feel especially appreciated when they receive special hand-made treats and take-home tokens of the gala event. From picture frames that double as place cards and will later hold a picture of the baby to the beautifully crafted cones of goodies that decorate chair backs to boxes of treats that dot the tables, these clever designs will hold special savories and add a festive flair as you celebrate and welcome the precious new addition into the lives of his or her parents, family, and friends.

Baby Shower Favors

Picture Perfect Frame

Materials

- Acrylic paint
- Adhesives: craft glue, glue stick
- Awl
- Cardstock: coordinating color
- Craft scissors
- Decorative paper: coordinating prints (2)
- Foam brush
- Name plate with brads
- Pencil
- Picture frame: wooden
- Ribbon: ⅜" coordinating pattern
- Ruler
- Sanding block

Instructions

1. Remove glass and back from frame; paint frame with acrylic paint and foam brush.

2. Using frame as template, cut one sheet of decorative paper to fit bottom two thirds of frame; cut coordinating paper to fit top third. Adhere with generous application of glue stick. Sand all edges smooth.

3. Tie 2' length of ribbon around sides of frame, covering edges where papers meet; trim excess. Center name plate on bottom of frame and mark holes; remove plate. Create holes for brads using awl. Apply small amount of craft glue in holes and affix name plate to frame with brads.

4. If desired, insert a photo of the baby on one side and the birth announcement or quote on the other.

time-saving tip

Write It Out

To save minutes, eliminate the name plate and replace the quote with the guest's name hand written on cardstock. Cut it to fit the frame opening and insert.

Marshmallow Lollipop

Materials

- Candy decorations: pastel-colored
- Cellophane
- Craft scissors
- Dipping chocolate
- Journaling pen
- Lollipop stick

- Marshmallow: large
- Ribbon: ⅜"
- Ruler
- Tag: mini
- Thread: white
- Wax paper

Instructions

1. Heat dipping chocolate according to package instructions. Insert lollipop stick in marshmallow. Dip marshmallow into prepared chocolate; sprinkle with candy decorations. Lay decorated marshmallow on wax paper; refrigerate until chocolate is hard.

2. Cut 9" square piece of cellophane. Loosely wrap around lollipop, gathering under marshmallow; wrap 12" length of ribbon around cellophane and tie into bow.

3. Write guest's name on mini-tag if desired; attach to ribbon with thread.

time-saving tip

Spread and Roll

Decorate chocolate-covered marshmallows quickly by rolling them in candy decorations that have been spread on a plate.

Just Ducky Box

Materials

- Adhesives: strong double-sided tape, tape runner
- Bone folder
- Cardstock: double-sided printed (2), white
- Cellophane bag: 6" square
- Craft scissors
- Die cut: yellow duck
- Filler: desired goodies
- Paper punch: decorative-edge
- Paper trimmer
- Ribbon: ¼"
- Ruler
- Self-adhesive hook-and-loop dot: ½" circle
- Stapler and staples

Instructions

1. **To make box:** Cut one sheet of printed cardstock to 6" x 12" using paper trimmer. Score and crease at 2¼", 6¼", and 8¼" using bone folder. Fold short end to outside of tent.

2. **To make topper:** Cut second sheet of printed cardstock to 6" x 5". Score and crease at 2½" x 6". Cut two pieces of white cardstock to 6" x 1"; edge one 6" side of each with decorative-edge paper punch. Adhere white cardstock to underside of each 6" side of topper; attach topper to folded tent using tape runner. Tie ribbon around duck die cut and attach to topper with double-sided tape.

3. Fill cellophane bag with goodies. Fold over top 2"; secure with staples. Adhere one side of fold next to top crease inside tent with double-sided tape.

4. Center hook-and-loop dot under front flap. *Note:* Keep both parts of hook-and-loop dot together and apply to one side of the flap, then close and press for perfect alignment.

Sweet as a Daisy

Materials

- Adhesives: tape runner, thick craft glue
- Craft scissors
- Decorative paper: coordinating prints (2)
- Die-cut tool and die: oval tag
- Foam cube: 3"
- Inkpad: coordinating color
- Journaling pen
- Paper trimmer
- Pencil
- Ribbon: ⅜"
- Ruler
- Silk flower: gerbera daisy with stem
- Spanish moss

Instructions

1. Cut five 3" squares from one sheet of decorative paper using paper trimmer; ink all edges. Adhere to four sides and bottom of foam cube using tape runner.

2. Make deep hole in center top of cube using pencil; insert gerbera flower stem. Apply generous amount of craft glue to top of cube; adhere Spanish moss.

3. Die-cut oval tag from second sheet of decorative paper; ink edges. Write guest's name on tag with journaling pen, if desired. Tie to stem with ribbon; trim excess.

time-saving tip

Keep It Under Wrap

Consider leaving the plastic wrap on the foam cube and adhering decorative paper with a tape runner.

Kisses for Baby

Materials

- Adhesive: cellophane tape
- Cardstock
- Cellophane bag: 3" x 4"
- Chocolate kisses (7)
- Computer and printer
- Craft scissors
- Fabric flower: 2½"
- Hole punch: ¼"
- Paper punch: corner rounder
- Printed transparency overlay
- Ribbon: ¼" picot-edged
- Rubber band
- Ruler

Instructions

1. Cut transparency to 1½" x 6". Wrap into cylinder shape, overlapping ¼"; secure with tape. Insert cylinder in cellophane bag; tape bag corners to underside of cylinder.

2. Fill bag with chocolate kisses; secure top with rubber band. Fold flower in half and cut ⅛" slit in center; insert gathered cellophane through slit in flower center.

3. Cut cardstock to 1" x 2" to create tag; trim corners with corner rounder. If desired, print name or message on tag using computer. Punch hole near top middle of tag, then cut small "V" in hole. Place tag on top of flower. Tie 6" length of ribbon to flower and tag to secure.

time-saving tip

Hand-Write Your Words

Use pre-made shipping tags and write your special message rather than using a computer to print the words to speed the production of the Kisses for Baby party favors.

Paper Cone

Materials

- Adhesives: glue dot, strong double-sided tape, tape runner
- Bone folder
- Decorative paper: double-sided
- Filler: desired goodies
- Hole punch: ¼"
- Inkpads: coordinating colors (2)
- Paper trimmer
- Pencil
- Ribbon: ⅜" printed grosgrain, 1" organdy
- Scissors: craft, decorative-edge
- Shredded paper

Instructions

1. Copy Paper Cone Template (page 120); trace onto decorative paper and cut out using paper trimmer. Score on dashed lines using bone folder and crease. Fold small triangle toward outside and long triangles toward each other; adhere overlap with double-sided tape.

2. Trim edge of front triangle with decorative-edge scissors; ink edges of flap. Punch two holes on opposite sides ½" down from top of cone.

3. Tie 12" length of grosgrain ribbon into bow; adhere to flap with glue dot. Apply tape runner to back of remaining 18" length of grosgrain ribbon; layer onto 18" length of organdy ribbon. Thread double ribbon through outside of hole toward inside of cone; tie knot. Repeat with opposite end of ribbon on opposite side of cone.

4. Fill with shredded paper and shower goodies.

time-saving tip

Go for Wider Ribbon

To save time, consider using a wider ribbon for the handle and skip layering the two ribbons.

Diaper Cup

Materials

- Adhesive: craft glue
- Bead: small
- Fabric: flannel
- Filler: mints or other candies
- Flower: small paper
- Paper condiment cup: 2"
- Pinking shears
- Ruler
- Safety pin: $\frac{1}{2}$"

Instructions

1. Cut 7" square of flannel using pinking shears; fold into triangle "diaper."

2. With folded edge toward top, wrap diaper sides around cup. Fold triangle flap up to front; secure with safety pin through all fabric layers. *Note:* A simple tag with the guest's name could be added to the pin embellishment to personalize the favor, if desired.

3. Embellish diaper pin with small flower and bead. Fill cup with mints or other candies.

time-saving tip

Diaper Pin Decor
Use a pre-decorated diaper pin to embellish the front of the diaper cup. Or, rather than glue the beads to the favor, thread them onto the safety pin.

Coupon Booklet

Materials

- Adhesives: foam dots, tape runner
- Bone folder
- Cardstock: coordinating colors (2)
- Computer and printer
- Cosmetic sponge
- Decorative paper: coordinating prints (2)
- Diaper pin
- Hole punch: $\frac{1}{4}$"
- Inkpad: coordinating color
- Paper trimmer
- Ribbon: $\frac{3}{8}$" gingham
- Ruler
- Scissors: craft, decorative-edge

Instructions

1. **To make booklet:** Cut one sheet of cardstock to 12" x 2½" using paper trimmer. Cut one sheet of decorative paper to 12" x 2"; center and adhere to cardstock strip using tape runner. Score and fold at 1¼" from left end and 5" from right end.

2. **To make coupons:** Using computer, print "Coupons for You" onto second sheet of decorative paper; cut to 3" x 1¼" using paper trimmer. Print six coupons in 5½" x 2¼" text boxes onto decorative paper, leaving left 1½" of each text box free of text. Cut out text boxes with decorative-edge scissors. Cut piece of cardstock to 3" x 1¼" using paper trimmer; adhere behind "Coupons for You" text box, and then ink edges. Adhere title to front of booklet with foam dots. Cut six pieces of cardstock to 5½" x 2¼" using paper trimmer; adhere behind coupons, and then ink edges.

3. Stack coupons and tuck into left edge of booklet. Punch two holes with ¼" hole punch ½" from fold and ½" from top and bottom. *Note:* You may need to punch through the cover then mark and punch holes in coupons one at a time to achieve perfect alignment.

4. Thread 12" length of ribbon through holes; tie bow on front. Embellish with diaper pin.

Chris and Sarah

CHAPTER 5

Your guests will be elated when they receive wedding favors "to have and to hold" as their very own. Beautifully handcrafted trinkets will bring back fond memories of this special day long after the ceremony is over. These gifts will remind guests of the importance of their presence and serve as a special thank you for their attendance. Whether you choose a votive personalized with excerpts from the wedding vows, a handmade wire and glass bud vase, a napkin ring featuring a photo of the couple that converts to a magnet, or a delightful scroll with a sincere message of thanks, you'll add to the celebration and make your guests feel very special as they share in the significance of this important day.

Tears of Joy Packet

Materials

- Adhesive: tape runner
- Cardstock: double-sided printed, white
- Charm: monogram letter for couple's last name
- Computer and printer
- Eyelet setting tools
- Eyelets (2)
- Paper punch: corner rounder
- Paper trimmer
- Ribbon: $\frac{3}{8}$"
- Ruler
- Scissors: craft, decorative-edge
- Scoring tool
- Tissues

Instructions

1. Cut printed cardstock to 3"x 7" using paper trimmer; score and fold at 4½" from top edge. Trim edge of short section with decorative-edge scissors.

2. Secure front to back by setting eyelets near upper edge of front section, creating pocket. Finish upper edges of back using corner rounder.

3. Thread 10" length of ribbon through eyelets, and then thread charm onto ribbon and knot.

4. Using computer, print desired message on white cardstock, if desired. Trim text to 2½"x ½" and mat with double-sided cardstock; adhere to lower edge of pocket with tape runner.

5. Fold one or two pieces of tissue into fourths and tuck into pocket.

time-saving tip

An Alternate Closure

Eliminate the eyelets and apply a small amount of adhesive to the inside edges to keep the tissue pocket closed. Then wrap ribbon completely around the pocket, securing it at the back with a tape runner.

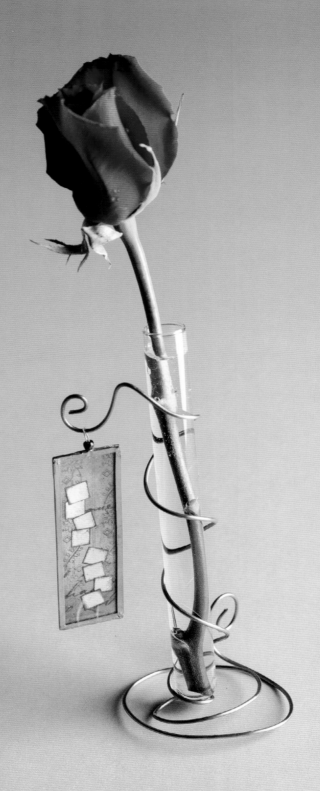

True Love Vase

Materials

- Adhesive: glue stick
- Bead: glass
- Copper tape: ¼" self-adhesive
- Craft scissors
- Decorative paper: double-sided
- Dowel: ¾"
- Glass slide: 1"x 3"
- Inkpad: coordinating color
- Journaling pen (optional)
- Pencil
- Ruler
- Scrap paper
- Test tube: 6"
- Wire: 14-gauge copper, 26-gauge copper
- Wire pliers

Instructions

1. Create small spiral in first 2" of 2' piece of 14-gauge wire. Twist large spiral in next 12"; bend first spiral vertically and second spiral horizontally, creating 3" base. Wrap wire around test tube with three twists to reach the top. Twist remaining wire into small spiral and bend away from edge of test tube, creating a hanger.

2. Using glass slide as a template, trace and cut decorative paper rectangle. Cut out small squares and ink edges. Adhere squares to decorative paper. Lay paper behind glass slide; wrap edges of slide with self-adhesive copper tape. Twist 2" of 26-gauge wire in small loop, and then twist together three times; thread bead over twist. Spread ends of wire apart and across top of slide; trim excess with wire pliers and then secure with copper tape.

3. Hand-write thank you message to guest on back of slide, if desired.

time-saving tip

Shaping Wire
Using a ¾" dowel to shape wire around will make the wire easier to handle and you won't have to worry about breaking the glass.

Special Delivery Box

Materials

- Adhesives: glue dots, tape runner, vellum tape
- Bone folder
- Cardstock: double-sided printed
- Charm: open heart
- Computer and printer
- Hole punch: ¼"

- Inkpad: coordinating color
- Paper trimmer
- Ribbon: ⅜" coordinating color
- Self-adhesive hook-and-loop dot: ½" circle
- Vellum

Instructions

1. Copy Special Delivery Box Template (page 122) onto cardstock; cut out using paper trimmer and then score on dotted lines according to template. Crease cardstock and then ink edges.

2. Using computer, print message onto vellum. Carefully tear around message so it measures approximately 8"x 5".

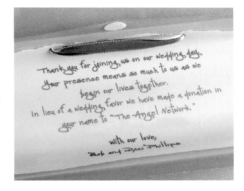

3. Lay vellum inside box with top of message on section marked for holes. Tack in place using vellum tape between hole marks. Punch holes through vellum and box as indicated on template.

4. Thread charm onto ribbon. Thread ribbon from outside of box to inside. Cross ribbons and then thread back to outside of box. Adjust ribbon ends and secure with glue dots; trim ends. Secure charm with glue dot if needed.

5. Position and adhere hook-and-loop dot to underside of flap and to outside of second section, creating five-sided box.

Goblet Charm

Materials

- Beads: small glass
- Computer and printer
- Craft scissors
- Decorative paper
- Hole punch: 1/16"
- Pencil
- Ruler
- Tag rim: 1" heart
- Wire: 24-gauge
- Wire pliers

Instructions

1. **To create tag:** Using computer, print name of guest for one side of tag and name of couple and wedding date to fit inside opposite side of tag onto decorative paper, if desired. Using rim as template, trace and cut around names; insert into tag and crimp edges closed. Punch hole in upper lobe of heart.

2. Make small curl in one end of wire using wire pliers. Thread 4" of beads onto wire. Slide tag on wire, leaving 1/4" gap from end of beads. Neatly twist wire back onto itself; trim excess.

time-saving tip

Stamp Instead of Print

Stamp names of guests onto ready-made tags instead of computer printing and inserting into tag rims.

Mini-Collage Napkin Ring

Materials

- Adhesives: ¼" strong double-sided tape, cellophane tape, foam tape, tape runner
- Cardstock: double-sided printed
- Computer and printer
- Craft scissors
- Favor tin: 2" lid with clear window
- Inkpad: coordinating color
- Journaling pen: black
- Magnet: self-adhesive
- Mini-marbles: crystal transparent (½ tsp.)
- Paper punch: ¼" heart
- Pencil
- Photograph
- Ribbon: ⅜" velvet
- Ruler

Instructions

1. Using outside of lid as template, trace and cut photo and one circle from double-sided cardstock; adhere back of photo to circle using double-sided tape.

2. Cut 1" x ¼" strip of cardstock. Write "Love" with journaling pen on strip; ink edges and adhere to photo using foam tape.

3. Punch six tiny hearts from cardstock; place in upside-down lid. Pour ½ tsp. of mini-marbles into lid. Lay photo on back of lid; secure with small pieces of cellophane tape around edges.

4. Apply double-sided tape around edges of lid; adhere velvet ribbon.

5. Cut strip of cardstock to 6" x 2". Fold in half lengthwise; adhere with tape runner to create 6" x 1" strip; ink edges. Using computer, print "Cut ring to use as magnet" in small font; cut into strip and then adhere to center of cardstock strip. Shape into ring with text inside by overlapping ½"; secure with double-sided tape. Apply 1" strip of double-sided tape to outside of ring at overlap; adhere to back side of collaged lid. Adhere magnet inside ring directly under collage.

CD Holder

Materials

- Adhesives: craft glue, double-side tape
- Beaded embellishment
- Cardstock: white embossed
- CD label
- CD of choice
- Computer and printer
- Copy paper
- Craft scissors
- Inkpad: silver
- Metal-edged vellum tag: 1½" square
- Paper trimmer
- Pencil
- Ribbon: 3" iridescent
- Rubber stamps: wedding-themed
- Ruler
- Scoring tool

Instructions

1. Copy CD Holder Template (page 123) onto cardstock. Cut on solid lines according to template; score and fold on broken lines. Fold narrow flaps to inside; fold and adhere lower half to flaps, creating 5"-square pocket.

2. Wrap 12" length of ribbon around width of pocket; secure in back center with double-sided tape. Adhere beaded embellishment to front of pocket with craft glue.

3. Using computer, print title on copy paper. Cut to fit behind vellum tag, and then tuck tag under edge of embellishment and adhere.

4. Stamp CD label with images using silver inkpad.

time-saving tip

Print out Labels

Print purchased CD labels according to package instructions rather than hand-stamping them.

Wedding Bookmark

Materials

- Adhesives: cellophane tape, tape runner
- Cardstock: double-sided printed, white
- Charms: silver (2)
- Inkpad: coordinating color
- Paper punch: corner rounder
- Paper trimmer
- Ribbon: 1" organdy
- Ruler
- Scissors: craft, decorative-edge
- Wire: 26-gauge silver
- Wire pliers

Instructions

1. Thread 18" length of ribbon through charm, folding 1" back onto itself. Tightly wrap 12" length of wire around overlapped ribbon eight times; closely trim excess wire and ribbon. Repeat on opposite end with remaining charm.

2. Cut printed cardstock to 7"x 1¼" using paper trimmer; ink edges. With decorative-edge scissors, cut white cardstock to 7"x 1½"; layer and adhere strips together using tape runner, with decorative edge extending beyond edges of paper strip. Cut printed cardstock to 3"x 9" using paper trimmer; round corners and ink edges.

3. Fold ribbon so one end is longer than the other. Bend ribbon fold over top end of large rectangle; secure on backside with cellophane tape. Wrap paper strip around display card, creasing at edges to create band; secure with cellophane tape.

time-saving tip

Part of the Décor

For a clever presentation, personalize the bookmark and lay it across your guest's plate or tuck into his or her napkin ring, eliminating the need for a placecard.

Lighted Votive

Materials

- Adhesives: glue dot, vellum tape
- Charm: double heart
- Computer and printer
- Craft scissors
- Glass candle votive: triangular
- Glass gems: clear
- Leafing pen: gold
- Light: miniature battery-operated
- Pencil
- Scrap paper
- Spray crackle medium: off-white, two-step gold
- Thread: gold metallic
- Vellum

Instructions

1. Using computer, print names of couple and phrases from wedding vows on three sections of vellum. Spray lightly with gold crackle medium according to manufacturer's instructions, avoiding text as much as possible; let dry. Lightly spray with off-white crackle medium.

2. Trace side of votive onto scrap paper; cut inside line to create template. Trace template onto printed areas of vellum; cut out. Edge vellum lightly with gold leafing pen; adhere to sides of votive with vellum tape.

3. Wrap votive with strands of gold metallic thread, stringing through heart charm. *Note:* Heart charm can be painted with gold leafing pen to change the color, if desired.

4. Place glue dot on back corner of votive. Run thread across glue dot to secure.

5. Fill votive with glass gems; turn on light according to package instructions and push into center of gems.

time-saving tip

Real Flame Glow

In place of the battery-operated light and gems, consider inserting a votive candle.

CHAPTER 6

The decorations are in place, the tables are set, the ambiance is just as you had imagined, and the guests are about to arrive. What a special moment when you are handed a beautifully handmade or elegantly wrapped hostess gift. On the pages that follow you will find ideas for thank you gifts that can be personalized to match the event or coordinate with the décor in your hostess's home. Gifts to relax with after the event winds down are especially welcomed by the party giver, as are offerings that will bring beauty to the hostess's home or garden in the coming days or months. These projects are sure to be greatly appreciated and can be handmade in only minutes.

Hostess Gifts

Stationery Set

Materials

- Adhesive: tape runner
- Blank note cards and envelopes (4)
- Cardstock: copper, double-sided printed
- Chalks: coordinating colors
- Charm: metal
- Craft scissors
- Decorative paperclip
- Embossing powder: clear
- Heat tool

- Hole punches: $1/4$", $1/2$"
- Inkpads: pigment ink in coordinating colors
- Leafing pen: copper
- Paper trimmer
- Ribbon: $3/8$" grosgrain
- Rubber stamps: coordinating images
- Ruler
- Scoring tool

Instructions

1. **To create folder:** Cut piece of double-sided cardstock to 12" x 9¾" using paper trimmer; score down center of 12" width and up 2½" from bottom edge. Fold paper inside out; cut long narrow triangle ¼" from center fold of bottom section, angled to intersection of scored lines. Fold flaps up to inside of holder; adhere with tape runner along outer edges. Fold on center line to form folder. Stamp images on inside and outside with coordinating chalks.

2. Punch two ¼" holes side by side in center edge of front cover. Thread 26" length of ribbon through holes, leaving 8" extending from right hole and 18" from left hole. Thread charm onto ribbon; position next to left hole. Adhere ribbon using tape runner.

time-saving tip

Change the Cover
To create the cover more quickly, simplify the label by eliminating the mat layers or use stickers instead.

Above: Simple stamped images coordinate the one-of-a-kind cards with their envelopes. **Opposite:** Using a themed stamp set allows you to create a group of cards, each unique yet coordinating.

3. Cut three triangular pieces of cardstock varying sizes. Edge sides with copper leafing pen. Stack and adhere to front of folder over ribbon; embellish with decorative paperclip.

4. Create five copper cardstock embellishments by punching ½" holes, and then punching ¼" holes inside. Adhere along right edge of front cover.

5. To make notecards: Cut four pieces of white cardstock to 2¼" x 3". Stamp images with pigment ink, and then sprinkle with clear embossing powder; melt with heat tool. Mat with two layers of coordinating cardstock. Adhere to front of cards with tape runner. Stamp image onto flaps of four envelopes. Place cards and envelopes in folder pockets. Tie closed with ribbon.

time-saving tip

Stamp to Save Minutes

To make this a quick and easy gift to create, replace embossed images with dye ink-stamped images.

Wildflower Decanter

Materials

- Adhesives: glue dot, tape runner
- Button
- Craft scissors
- Decanter: small
- Decorative paper
- Floss: brown (18")
- Inkpad: coordinating color
- Journaling pen: black
- Paper trimmer
- Ribbon: $\frac{3}{8}$" wide (20")
- Tag: jewelry-size
- Vellum
- Wildflower seeds

Instructions

1. Fill decanter with wildflower seeds. Cut vellum to 5"x 2" using paper trimmer; write personal message on vellum and tear edges. Roll message into scroll; wrap with floss and tie, leaving one end 3" long.

2. Ink edges of jewelry tag; inscribe with guest's name and tie to long end of floss. Insert scroll into decanter with tag extending to outside.

3. Cut decorative paper to 8"x 1¼" using paper trimmer; ink edges. Adhere paper strip around center of jar using tape runner. Cut ribbon in half; adhere one half over top of decanter to center of band on each side. *Note:* This step can be eliminated if the lid is secure.

4. Adhere remaining ribbon half around center of band, extending 1" past end of band; trim into "V." Tie floss through holes in button; knot. Adhere button to ribbon with glue dot.

time-saving tip

Choose Your Bottle Carefully

Purchase bottles with tight lids to eliminate the need for placing ribbon over the top to secure.

Coaster Set

Materials

- Cardstock: coordinating color, cream
- Ceramic tiles (4)
- Cork: self-adhesive shelf liner
- Cosmetic sponges
- Craft scissors
- Heat tool
- Hole punch: ¼"
- Inkpads: permanent coordinating colors (2-3)
- Journaling pen
- Paper towel
- Raffia
- Rubber stamp
- Ruler

Instructions

1. Clean tiles with wet paper towel; let dry. Apply ink to edges and surface of tile using cosmetic sponge. *Note:* Use light-colored ink on surface where you'll be stamping an image.

2. Stamp image with darker ink onto face of tiles; set with heat tool.

3. Cut four pieces of cork shelf liner into 3½" squares; peel away backing, then adhere to underside of tile.

4. Cut cream cardstock to ⅝" x 3". Stamp with section of image to coordinate with coasters; ink edges. Cut coordinating cardstock to ⅞" x 3¼"; ink edges. Layer rectangles then punch hole at top end of both layers.

5. Stack coasters and wrap with raffia; attach tags and tie raffia into bow.

time-saving tip

Dry Coasters Faster

When making many sets of coasters, lay inked tiles on a cookie sheet and place in an oven at 200 degrees for 10 minutes instead of setting ink with a heat tool.

Pamper Kit

Materials

- Acrylic paint
- Adhesive: glue stick
- Box: 9" x 4½" x 4½" unfinished chipboard
- Decorative paper
- Filler: bath salts, body lotion, candies, candles, towel
- Foam brush
- Foam stamp: large flourish
- Inkpad: black
- Paper trimmer
- Stickers: 2" alphabet

Instructions

1. Open box and lay flat. Paint foam stamp with acrylic paint and foam brush; stamp flourishes on box.

2. Cut decorative paper to 4½" x 2" using paper trimmer. Tear top edge; adhere under stamped word. Cut two 4½" squares of decorative paper. Ink edges, and then adhere one to underside of lid and one to lid top.

3. Fill box with suggested items. *Note:* Leaving the box open will allow more room for fillers and will provide an appealing presentation.

time-saving tip

Apply Paint with Ease

Using paint-filled dabbers when stamping with foam stamps will aid in the speed and neatness of applying paint to projects.

Bottle Gift Box

Materials

- Acrylic paint: copper
- Adhesive: glue stick
- Cardstock: copper
- Craft scissors
- Decorative paper: double-sided (2)
- Embossing powder: copper
- Foam brush
- Foam stamps: coordinating (2)
- Heat tool
- Hole punch: ¼"
- Inkpads: copper, white
- Paper trimmer
- Pencil
- Ribbon: 1" organdy
- Rubber stamp: desired message
- Ruler
- Wine gift box
- Wire: 24-gauge copper
- Wire pliers

Instructions

1. Paint all edges of gift box with acrylic paint using foam brush; let dry. Repeat with second coat if necessary.

2. Measure box height and circumference. Cut decorative paper accordingly, trimming paper slightly smaller than box to allow copper paint to show on edges; adhere to box with glue stick. Stamp outside of box with foam stamp and white ink. *Note:* Two or more coordinating prints may be used to add interest.

3. Using top of box as template, trace and cut paper to cover top and bottom; adhere with glue stick. If inside of box will be exposed, measure and cut decorative paper to cover; adhere.

4. **To create band for box:** Cut 1"-wide decorative paper strip to fit circumference of box; adhere around center. Punch ¼" circles from copper cardstock; adhere at 1" intervals around band. Cut two pieces of copper cardstock to 1" square; adhere to ends of band where box opens. Punch ¼" circles in center of squares. Knot ribbon at one end and thread through hole with knot on inside of box; repeat with opposite side.

5. Create tag by stamping and embossing desired message in copper onto scrap of decorative paper; attach to ribbon with twisted copper wire.

Vanilla Extract

Materials

- Adhesive: glue stick
- Burnishing tool
- Cardstock: coordinating color
- Computer and printer
- Decorative bottle with cork
- Decorative paper
- Hole punches: ⅛", 1¾"
- Inkpad: coordinating color
- Rub-on transfer
- Ruler
- Twine
- Vanilla bean

Instructions

1. Apply rub-on transfer to front of bottle with burnishing tool.

2. Using computer, print recipe in 1½" diameter circle on cardstock. Punch out recipe and circle of decorative paper with 1¾" hole punch; adhere back to back, and then ink edges. Punch ⅛" hole in top of circle.

3. Wrap 18" length of twine several times around neck of bottle then through hole in tag and knot.

4. Insert vanilla bean into bottle and top with cork.

Recipe

Homemade Vanilla Extract

Slit vanilla bean and place in container. Fill with vodka and shake once a day for a week. Leave container in dark place for 2-3 months. Enjoy!

time-saving tip

Produce in Quantity

Rather than making one at a time, produce a large quantity of homemade vanilla extract recipe tags to have on hand to make hostess gifts quickly.

Set of Napkins

Materials

- Adhesive: tape runner
- Cardstock: double-sided printed, neutral-colored
- Cloth napkins (3-5)
- Craft scissors
- Decorative brad
- Hole punch: ⅛"
- Inkpads: chalk ink, fabric ink
- Iron
- Paper punch: corner rounder
- Paper trimmer
- Rubber or foam stamp: large
- Ruler
- Sticker: 1" monogram

Instructions

1. Open napkin and stamp large image with fabric ink in bottom right corner; let dry. Repeat with remaining napkins. Press back of napkins with dry iron to set ink. Fold each napkin to 5" x 10", and then stack together.

2. **To create band:** Cut strip of double-sided cardstock to 12" x 1"; ink edges using chalk ink. Cut neutral-colored cardstock to 1¼" square and round corners; ink edges. Apply monogram letter sticker toward right side of square. Adhere square to center of band. Punch ⅛" hole through both layers at left side of square; insert decorative brad, then open prongs to secure.

3. Wrap napkin stack with decorative band; adhere ends together where they over-lap at back of stack.

time-saving tip

Expand Napkin Choices

Wrap pre-printed napkins with the decorative band for a quick and easy alternative to stamping by hand.

Garden Party Bulb

Materials

- Bone folder
- Cardstock: light brown kraft
- Computer and printer
- Cosmetic sponge
- Craft scissors
- Daffodil bulb
- Decorative paper
- Inkpad: dye ink in olive green
- Metal-rimmed tag
- Paper punch: ¼" circle
- Pencil
- Rubber stamps: alphabet, garden-themed images
- Ruler
- Spanish moss
- Twill tape

Instructions

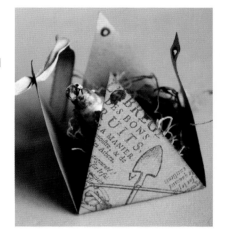

1. Copy Garden Party Bulb Template (page 124) and trace onto cardstock; cut out and score on solid lines. Stamp randomly with garden-themed stamps.

2. Punch hole near top of each flap. Ink edges of box and metal-rimmed tag using cosmetic sponge. Stamp guest's name onto strip of cardstock; adhere to tag.

3. Place bulb inside of box on nest of Spanish moss and assemble box.

4. Using computer, print instructions for planting onto decorative paper and place inside box. Thread twill tape through all holes and tag; tie with knot.

time-saving tip

Producing in Quantity

To save time when making a significant number of Garden Party Bulb favors, stamp several sheets of cardstock with garden images before cutting out the templates.

Templates

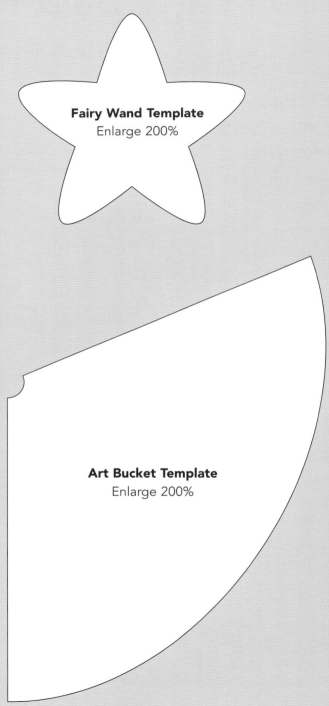

Fairy Wand Template
Enlarge 200%

Art Bucket Template
Enlarge 200%

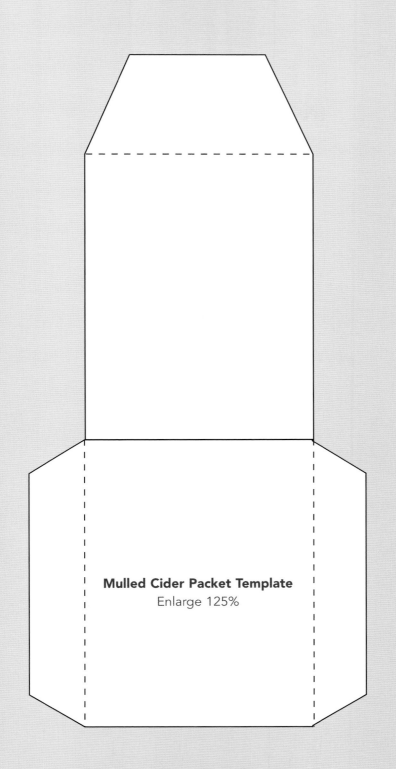

Mulled Cider Packet Template
Enlarge 125%

Templates

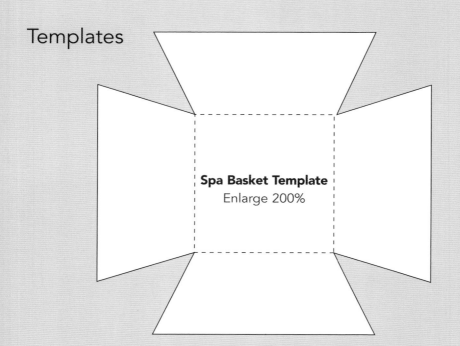

Spa Basket Template
Enlarge 200%

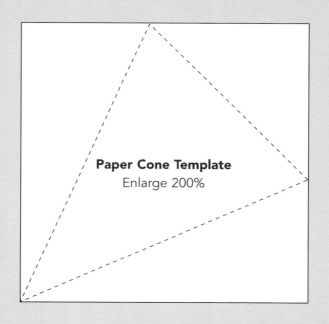

Paper Cone Template
Enlarge 200%

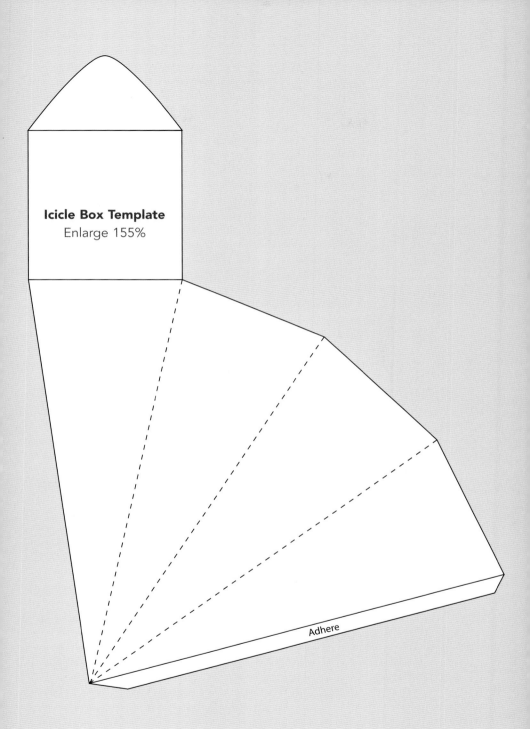

Icicle Box Template
Enlarge 155%

Adhere

Templates

Special Delivery Box Template
Enlarge 225%

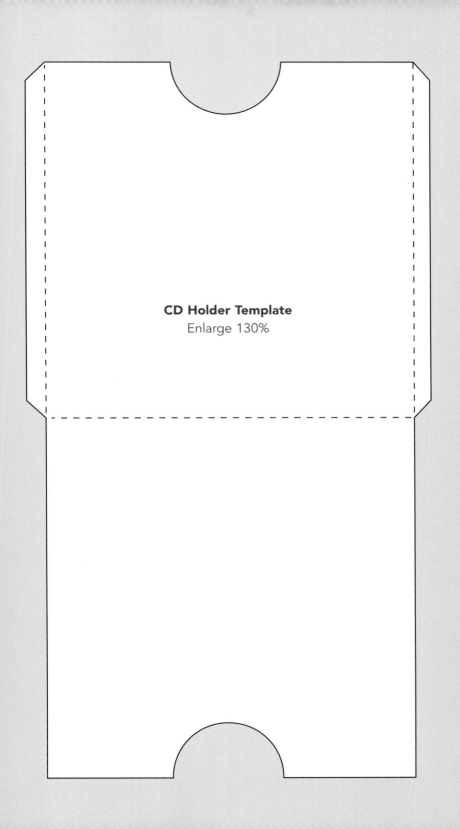

CD Holder Template
Enlarge 130%

Templates

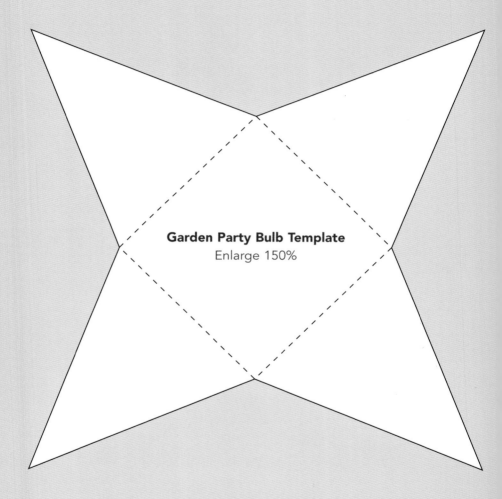

Garden Party Bulb Template
Enlarge 150%

About the Author

Roxi Phillips is an award-winning paper and mixed-media artist who has dabbled in a wide variety of crafts throughout her life. Her eclectic style and diversity is shown in her work, from altered art projects to more traditional scrapbooking.

Born and raised in the Pacific Northwest, Roxi developed a love of art in high school and has continued to nurture her talents by taking classes at local colleges and from visiting artists as well as attending conferences and symposiums. She taught preschool for 27 years, with an emphasis on learning through process-oriented art, and shared her passion for encouraging creativity in children with early childhood educators as a teacher-trainer.

Roxi designs paper arts projects using mixed media and scrapbooking techniques for several companies including Krylon® and Tapestry by CR Gibson®. Her work is featured regularly in national magazines such as *Altered Arts, Scrapbooking and Beyond*, *PaperCrafts*, and *PaperWorks* and crafting books including *Spray Paint Paper Crafts: Creative Fun with Krylon* (Sterling Publishing Co., Inc. © 2007). She is the author of *Make It in Minutes: Mini-Books* (Sterling Publishing Co., Inc. © 2006), and is a sought-after instructor of altered arts, book arts, and scrapbooking.

Roxi and her family live in western Tennessee.

Special Thanks

My family and friends are my constant sources of love and inspiration. It is only through their support and generosity that I can pursue my creative and artistic passions. They give me the strength to know I can do whatever I set my mind to, and for this I'm truly thankful.

Contributors

Shelly Hickox

Pages 44, 46, 54, 64, 82

A rubber stamp artist and paper crafter, Shelly Hickox's work has appeared in numerous publications including *Take Ten, Somerset Studio, Legacy, Stamper's Sampler* and *Altered Arts*. She resides in the beautiful countryside of northern Mississippi with her husband and two children.

Deb Kornrumpf

Page 24

Deb Kornrumpf is a banquet hall owner and party planner. She also is a muralist for VESTA home shows and the editor of *Portents* magazine. She and her husband live on a small farm in Tennessee with their six children.

Marci Lambert

Pages 34, 42, 72, 76, 108, 112, 114

Artist and photographer Marci Lambert's work has been seen in several major scrapbooking magazines including *Simple Scrapbooks, Creating Keepsakes, BHG Scrapbooks, Etc.*, and *Scrapbook Trends*. She was awarded with an Honorable Mention in the 2006 Creating Keepsakes Hall of Fame.

Candice Windham

Pages 28, 52, 68, 92, 100, 110

Graphic designer, painter, teacher, and paper artist Candice Windham is represented by the Rivertown Gallery in Memphis, Tennessee. She lives in Brighton, Tennessee with her husband, Larry, and dogs Pete and Sam.

METRIC EQUIVALENCY CHARTS

inches to millimeters and centimeters
(mm-millimeters, cm-centimeters)

inches	mm	cm	inches	cm	inches	cm
⅛	3	0.3	9	22.9	30	76.2
¼	6	0.6	10	25.4	31	78.7
½	13	1.3	12	30.5	33	83.8
⅝	16	1.6	13	33.0	34	86.4
¾	19	1.9	14	35.6	35	88.9
⅞	22	2.2	15	38.1	36	91.4
1	25	2.5	16	40.6	37	94.0
1¼	32	3.2	17	43.2	38	96.5
1½	38	3.8	18	45.7	39	99.1
1¾	44	4.4	19	48.3	40	101.6
2	51	5.1	20	50.8	41	104.1
2½	64	6.4	21	53.3	42	106.7
3	76	7.6	22	55.9	43	109.2
3½	89	8.9	23	58.4	44	111.8
4	102	10.2	24	61.0	45	114.3
4½	114	11.4	25	63.5	46	116.8
5	127	12.7	26	66.0	47	119.4
6	152	15.2	27	68.6	48	121.9
7	178	17.8	28	71.1	49	124.5
8	203	20.3	29	73.7	50	127.0

yards to meters

yards	meters	yards	meters	yards	meters	yards	meters	yards	meters
⅛	0.11	2⅛	1.94	4⅛	3.77	6⅛	5.60	8⅛	7.43
¼	0.23	2¼	2.06	4¼	3.89	6¼	5.72	8¼	7.54
⅜	0.34	2⅜	2.17	4⅜	4.00	6⅜	5.83	8⅜	7.66
½	0.46	2½	2.29	4½	4.11	6½	5.94	8½	7.77
⅝	0.57	2⅝	2.40	4⅝	4.23	6⅝	6.06	8⅝	7.89
¾	0.69	2¾	2.51	4¾	4.34	6¾	6.17	8¾	8.00
⅞	0.80	2⅞	2.63	4⅞	4.46	6⅞	6.29	8⅞	8.12
1	0.91	3	2.74	5	4.57	7	6.40	9	8.23
1⅛	1.03	3⅛	2.86	5⅛	4.69	7⅛	6.52	9⅛	8.34
1¼	1.14	3¼	2.97	5¼	4.80	7¼	6.63	9¼	8.46
1⅜	1.26	3⅜	3.09	5⅜	4.91	7⅜	6.74	9⅜	8.57
1½	1.37	3½	3.20	5½	5.03	7½	6.86	9½	8.69
1⅝	1.49	3⅝	3.31	5⅝	5.14	7⅝	6.97	9⅝	8.80
1¾	1.60	3¾	3.43	5¾	5.26	7¾	7.09	9¾	8.92
1⅞	1.71	3⅞	3.54	5⅞	5.37	7⅞	7.20	9⅞	9.03
2	1.83	4	3.66	6	5.49	8	7.32	10	9.14

INDEX

A babe in the house is a well-spring of pleasure, a messenger of peace and love, a resting place for innocence on earth, a link between angels and men

Martin Farquhar Tupper